...time for soul

to stretch...

before the world

comes back on it.

Louis MacNeice

i live my life in widening circles
that reach out across the world.

Rainer Maria Rilke

stretch out your hand
and receive the world's
wide gift of joy,
appreciation and beauty.

Corinne Roosevelt Robinson

the body is your temple.
keep it pure and clean
for the soul to reside in.

B.K.S. Iyengar

the conclusion is always the same: love is the most powerful and still the most unknown energy of the world.

Pierre Teilhard de Chardin

if your compassion
does not include yourself,
it is incomplete.

Jack Kornfield

person to person,
moment to moment,
as we love, we change the world.

Samahria Lyte Kaufman

it is life itself
that must be our practice.

Diane Mariechild